# Pie for Piglets
## Counting by Twos

Special thanks to our advisers for their expertise:

Stuart Farm, M.Ed., Mathematics Lecturer
University of North Dakota, Grand Forks

Susan Kesselring, M.A., Literacy Educator
Rosemount-Apple Valley-Eagan (Minnesota) School District

by Michael Dahl    illustrated by Todd Ouren

PICTURE WINDOW BOOKS
Minneapolis, Minnesota

Managing Editor: Catherine Neitge
Creative Director: Terri Foley
Art Director: Keith Griffin
Editor: Christianne Jones
Designer: Todd Ouren
Page production: Picture Window Books
The illustrations in this book were prepared digitally.

Picture Window Books
5115 Excelsior Boulevard
Suite 232
Minneapolis, MN 55416
877-845-8392
www.picturewindowbooks.com

Printed in the United States of America.

Library of Congress Cataloging-in-Publication Data
Dahl, Michael.
Pie for piglets : counting by twos / written By Michael Dahl;
illustrated by Todd Ouren.
p. cm. — (Know your numbers)
ISBN 1-4048-0943-0 (hardcover)
1. Counting—Juvenile literature. 2. Multiplication—Juvenile
literature. 3. Piglets—Juvenile literature. I. Ouren, Todd, ill.
II. Title.

QA113.D35 2005
513.2'11—dc22                    2004018521

Two hungry piglets were home alone.
"Pie! Pie!" they piped.
"Let's make pie!"

Sty
Swe
Sty

# The piglets put in TWO sacks of flour.

4

5

The piglets put in FOUR sticks of creamy butter.

2 4

Sty Sweet Sty

7

The piglets put in SIX cobs
of golden corn.

Slop

2 4 6

8

9

The piglets put in EIGHT cups
of chocolate milk.

2 4 6 8

11

The piglets put in TEN gooey cinnamon rolls.

The piglets put in TWELVE Grade A eggs.

| 2 | 4 | 6 | 8 | 10 | 12 |

14

The piglets put in FOURTEEN mushy meatballs.

2 4 6 8 10 12 14

The piglets put in SIXTEEN
peanut butter sandwiches.

The piglets put in EIGHTEEN pieces
of pineapple pizza.

2  4  6  8  10  12  14  16  18

19

The piglets put in TWENTY scoops of hunky, chunky, funky ice cream.

| 2 | 4 | 6 | 8 | 10 | 12 | 14 | 16 | 18 | 20 |

Then the piglets began eating the pie.
"Yum! Yum!" they squealed.
"We made the perfect pie!"

Flour

Sugar

23

## Fun Facts

 The average pig eats 5 pounds (2.25 kilograms) of food each day.

A baby pig is called a piglet, a father pig is called a boar, and a mother pig is called a sow.

Pigs do not sweat. They don't have any sweat glands on their bodies.

Pigs are considered one of the smartest animals.

Pigs and hippopotamuses are cousins.

## On the Web

FactHound offers a safe, fun way to find Web sites related to this book. All of the sites on FactHound have been researched by our staff. *www.facthound.com*

1. Visit the FactHound home page.
2. Enter a search word related to this book, or type in this special code: 1404809430
3. Click on the FETCH IT button.

Your trusty FactHound will fetch the best Web sites for you!

24

## Find the Numbers

Now you have finished reading the story, but a surprise still awaits you. Hidden in each picture is a multiple of 2 from 2 to 20. Can you find them all?

**2**–on the boy pig's flour sack

**4**–on the boy pig's hoof

**6**–on the hat

**8**–on the milk carton

**10**–on the pie pan

**12**–on the egg carton

**14**–on the girl pig's bow

**16**–on the meatball near the center

**18**–on the top of the pizza

**20**–on the ice cream near the hat

## Look for all of the books in the Know Your Numbers series: